My Colorful Travels

Irish Flowers
Volume 1

A Greyscale Coloring Book of Flowers in Ireland

By Susan Bryson

ISBN-13: 978-1545549001
ISBN-10: 1545549001

Irish Flowers

When I first moved to Ireland it was the end of summer and many flowers were still in bloom. I was enamored with nature's beautiful colors against the many shades of green. The pictures in this book are of flowers I've seen both in the typical Irish garden and in the beautiful Irish countryside. I hope you enjoy them as much as I do.

There are forty-two images to color in this book.

Happy Coloring!

My Colorful Travels

By Susan Bryson

How to Color in Grayscale

1. Let the shading of the grayscale photo be your guide.

2. Using your preferred medium (colored pencils, colored pens or paint), use lighter colors in lighter shaded areas, medium colors in medium shaded areas and darker colors in darker shaded areas.

3. Color in the direction of the natural line of the flower, leaf, etc.

4. In some of the photos, there is more focus on the flower and the background can look unfocused. You can either leave the unfocused background as it is, or color it using the general guidelines above; For example, start with darker colors on darker areas, then use your lighter colors in the lighter shaded areas. Leave the edges jagged as you color. Then go back over the areas using your medium colors to blend it all together.

5. You can still color the darkest areas of the photo as it will help to bring the image to life and help it to blend in with the rest of the picture.

6. If still in doubt over how to color in your grayscale image, I recommend checking the Internet for helpful videos that will offer additional tips and advice on coloring in grayscale.

These tips are only a general guideline, please feel free to use your own initiative and creativity!

Use this page to test your colors and different coloring techniques

Azalea

Azalea

Bluebell

Blue-Eyed Grass

Cherry Blossom

Cherry Blossom

Clematis

Clematis

Clover

Clover

Common Foxglove

Common Foxglove

Daffodil

Daffodil

Daisy

Daisy

Dogwood

Dogwood

Field Scabious

Field Scabious

Furze

Geranium

Geranium

Grape Hyacinth

Hydrangea

Hydrangea

Irish Eyes

Irish-Eyes Coneflower

Magnolia

Magnolia

Pansy

Pansy

Peony

Peony

Rhododendron

Alpenrose Rhododendron

Rose

Rose

Sunflower

Sunflowers

Tulip

Tulips